Imperfectly

Devoted

30 Day Devotional for Moms

By

Bethany Cloyd

Imperfectly Devoted

© 2025 Bethany Cloyd

ISBN: 979-8-9933636-1-5 (e-book)
ISBN: 979-8-9933636-0-8 (pbk)

First paperback edition October 2025

Cover design by Bethany Cloyd

Published in the United States of America

For more from Bethany Cloyd, visit

www.imperfectlydevoted.com

*This book is lovingly dedicated to my four precious children —
Vyron, Liam, Loxley, and Linex.*

*Being your mom has been my greatest calling and the most
beautiful lesson of my life. You have taught me more about
love, patience, faith, and perseverance than I could have ever
learned on my own. Each of you makes me want to strive every
single day to be better — to grow, to pray harder, and to live a
life that points you toward Jesus.*

*My deepest prayer is that the example I set before you always
leads you closer to the Lord. Of all the dreams I hold for your
futures, the greatest one is this: that you know Him, love Him,
and one day walk through heaven's gates.*

*You are my greatest blessings, and this devotional is a
reflection of the journey God has placed me on through the gift
of being your mom.*

Contents

Introduction

Welcome, Mama.

I'm so grateful you're here, and I truly can't wait to walk with you through these next 30 days. My prayer is that this devotional becomes a quiet place of encouragement, truth, and grace in the middle of your beautiful but messy life.

More than anything, I want you to know this: **you are not alone.**

Yes, you have the Lord—our omnipresent help, our constant strength, and our source of peace. But you also have sisters in motherhood all around the world who are walking through the same hard things: the doubts, the meltdowns (ours and theirs), the guilt, the joy, and the sacred responsibility of raising little hearts toward Jesus.

I don't know about you, but it brings me comfort to know that someone else has felt what I'm feeling, faced what I'm facing—and made it through.

Over these next 30 days, I'll be sharing parts of my own journey as a mom of four—raising kids in the church, messing up more times than I can count, falling short, and leaning on God's grace again and again.

This isn't about perfection. It's about presence. It's about turning our eyes back to the Lord in the middle of laundry, tantrums, and the moments we wonder if we're doing any of this right.

You're not alone, Mama. And you are so deeply loved. Let's grow together

Day 1

Defeated

Today, you walked out of worship feeling more defeated than filled.

You barely caught a full sentence of the sermon. Not because you didn't want to—oh, how you wanted to—but because you were juggling diaper changes, handing out snacks, coloring pages, and whispering gentle corrections while trying to break up yet another sibling squabble.

You sat there, exhausted, doing your best to keep little hands busy and little voices quiet. And yet, you couldn't help but feel like every eye was on you. The glances, the sighs—you imagined them all, even if they weren't really there. You just wanted a moment to breathe, to worship, to hear a word that would pour strength into your weary soul.

Instead, you leave, staring out the car window, wondering why you even bother—why you go through the chaos of getting everyone dressed and out the door, only to feel like you've missed everything.

But then, a gentle truth rises in your heart.

You're planting seeds.

"I planted, Apollos watered, but God gave the increase." (1 Corinthians 3:6)

You are training them up in the way they should go (Proverbs 22:6), even when it feels like nothing is sinking in.

Mama, even though they're climbing over the pew and whispering a little too loud, they're watching.

They see you worshiping.

They hear the preacher's voice—even in fragments.

They're beginning to learn the rhythm of attending services: the songs, the prayers, the quiet moments. It may not look like it yet, but trust me... the seeds are taking root.

This is just a season.

One where quiet time with God may happen more during nap time or after bedtime stories.

One where your prayers are whispered through tired tears for more faith, more patience, and more wisdom.

And in this sacred season, don't forget to pray for the little ones who made you a mama. Yes, they push your buttons. Yes, they stretch you more than you thought possible. But they are gifts—beautiful, messy, grace-filled gifts from a good God who sees every single effort you're making.

You may feel like you walked away from worship with nothing today.

But the Lord saw a mama planting seeds—and that is no small thing.

Today's Prayer

Lord,

Today I walked out of worship feeling more drained than filled.

I tried, Lord—I really did. I wanted to worship, to hear from You, to soak in Your Word. But instead, I was calming cries, wiping faces, opening snack bags, and chasing little feet that couldn't sit still.

And yet, even in the chaos, I know You saw me.

You saw my effort, my heart, and the quiet desperation behind my tired eyes. Thank You for reminding me that this season of noisy worship and distracted listening is not wasted. I'm not failing—I'm planting seeds.

Lord, help me believe that truth when discouragement creeps in. Help me remember that even when I catch only fragments of the sermon, You can still speak to my heart. That even when my hands are full, my spirit can still be open to You.

Give me peace when I feel judged or unseen.

Give me strength when I feel like giving up.

And remind me—again and again—that showing up matters. That raising my children to know You is holy work, even if it doesn't feel holy in the moment.

You've called me to this.

You will equip me for this.

So today, I lay down the guilt, the shame, the feeling of defeat, and I choose to trust that You are at work in my heart—and in the hearts of my children—even in the chaos.

In Jesus' name,

Amen.

1 Corinthians 3:6-8

I planted, Apollos watered, but God gave the increase. So then neither he who plants is anything, nor he who waters, but God who gives the increase. Now he who plants and he who waters are one, and each one will receive his own reward according to his own labor.

Proverbs 22:6

Train up a child in the way he should go: And when he is old, he will not depart from it.

Day 2

Great Intentions

If you're anything like me, you want to start your day with God. You've set the alarm with the best intentions—hoping to sneak in a quiet moment with your Bible before the kids wake up and the day begins.

But then someone was up sick all night... or your body begs for just a few more minutes of sleep before the whirlwind of mom life begins.

I get it. I really do.

You long to begin your day in the Word—but more often than not, it doesn't happen. And you feel a little guilty about it. I've been there. I'm still there some days.

Because the truth is... some mornings, motherhood is just plain exhausting.

But here's what I want you to hear, Mama:

It's okay. You are not failing. You are human.

And that's exactly why we need Jesus. He didn't die for the perfect version of us—He came for us in our mess, our tiredness, and our inconsistency. He knows our heart.

You didn't get to where you are overnight, and you won't become who you're growing into overnight either. Growth is slow, steady, and grace-filled.

Yes—starting your day in God's Word is beautiful. But if that doesn't happen, the next best thing is to simply make space for Him somewhere in your day.

Nap time. Bedtime. In the carpool line.

If it matters to you—and I believe it does—you'll find the moments. And God will meet you in them.

But don't stop there. Build a relationship.

Talk to Him while folding laundry—thank Him for the little bodies that fill those clothes.

Pray while stirring dinner—thank Him for the provision that fills your table.

You don't need perfect words or an uninterrupted hour.

You just need a heart that turns toward Him, again and again.

Today's Prayer

Heavenly Father,

You see me.

In the tired eyes. In the unwashed dishes. In the chaos of a home filled with little voices and busy feet—you see me.

Thank You for Your grace that meets me here, even when I feel like I'm falling short.

Even when I miss my quiet time.

Even when the only prayer I manage is a whispered "Help me, Lord."

Remind me that You are near, not because of how perfectly I perform, but because of who You are—faithful, loving, and patient.

Help me to find You in the small, sacred moments today.

When I rock a child to sleep—be near.

When I fold the laundry—speak to me.

When I drive, cook, clean, and care—draw my heart back to Yours again and again.

IMPERFECTLY DEVOTED

I want more of You, Lord—not just in the quiet hours but in the loud, messy, in-between moments too.

Let my life be worship, and let my motherhood become the altar where I learn to lay myself down in love.

Thank You for loving me and for never growing tired of my tired prayers.

In Jesus' name,

Amen.

2 Timothy 1:3-4

I thank God, whom I serve with a pure conscience, as my forefathers did, as without ceasing I remember you in my prayers night and day, greatly desiring to see you, being mindful of your tears, that I may be filled with joy.

Lamentations 3:22–23

The steadfast love of the Lord never ceases; His mercies never come to an end; they are new every morning; great is your faithfulness.

Day 3

Feeling Alone

You feel it late at night, don't you?

That ache for connection.

Since becoming a mom, life has become so wrapped up in caring for your family that making time for friendships feels nearly impossible. Conversations become fewer, and slowly, the closeness fades. And there you are—alone with your thoughts, wishing for someone to talk to. Someone to understand.

Your baby just took their first step—your heart is bursting with joy, but also breaking a little. How did that tiny newborn suddenly become a one-year-old?

You want to celebrate, you want to process, and you just wish you had someone to share it all with.

Here's the truth, sweet Mama: friends are a blessing—but they are not your lifeline.

They may come and go, but you have Someone who will never leave your side.

When your heart is full, or when it's heavy, when you need advice, when you're unsure, when you feel like you're losing yourself in motherhood—you can bring it all to Him.

Your Heavenly Father listens. He cares. He wants to be the one you turn to first.

He is the source of wisdom. The giver of peace. The One who sees you when you feel unseen.

So instead of sitting in the sadness of feeling alone like I often have, shift your gaze to things above.

Pour your heart out to the Lord—about the milestones, the meltdowns, the marriage struggles, the victories and the tears.

Be present with your beautiful family.

Cling to the One who never changes.

Let your contentment be found in Christ and the precious little ones He's entrusted to you.

Because even in the loneliest seasons, you are never truly alone, and those seasons are the best opportunity for growth in you.

Today's Prayer

Father,

In the quiet of the night, when the world is still and my thoughts are loud, I bring You my heart. You see the ache I carry—the longing for connection, for understanding, for someone to share this journey with. Lord, You know how easy it is to feel forgotten when my days are filled with wiping tears, folding laundry, and giving every ounce of myself to the ones I love.

But You, God... You see me.

You see my joy when my baby takes their first step. You see my tears when I feel overwhelmed and alone. You walk with me in every milestone and meltdown. You hear the silent prayers I whisper between diaper changes and dishes. You are the Friend who never leaves; the Comforter who always stays.

Help me, Lord, to turn to You first—to bring my thoughts, my celebrations, and my struggles to Your feet. Fill the empty spaces in my heart with Your peace and presence. Remind me that I don't have to carry this alone. Remind me that You are more than enough.

Thank You for entrusting these little souls to me. Help me to find joy in the simple, sacred work of motherhood and to know deep in my soul that I am never truly alone.

In Jesus' name,

Amen.

John 16:33

These things I have spoken to you, that in Me you may have peace. In the world you will have tribulation; but be of good cheer, I have overcome the world.

Isaiah 41:10

Fear not, for I am with you; Be not dismayed, for I am your God. I will strengthen you, yes, I will help you, I will uphold you with My righteous right hand.

Day 4

Does Anyone Listen?

The kids are finally home from school—you've missed them all day, and you're eager to reconnect, to hear their little voices tell you all about their day. But when you ask, all you get are the usual one-word answers:

"How was school?"

"Good."

"What did you do?"

"Stuff."

And just like that, they're off. Off to the toys, the snacks, the screens. You understand—they've been sitting still, following rules, and keeping their emotions in check all day. Now they're in their safe space, and they just want to be.

Then comes dinner.

You've poured time, energy, and love into this meal. You call them in—once, twice—and still no one comes.

Finally, they trickle in, arguing over seats, cups, and who gets to pray.

The bickering escalates, your patience thins, and suddenly you're snapping:

"CAN'T WE JUST HAVE ONE NICE FAMILY DINNER?!"

You didn't mean to yell.

You're tired.

You just wanted one peaceful moment.

You wonder why they listen so well at school and come home only to give you their most challenging behavior. I used to ask myself that all the time. Until one day, after a particularly rough day, I called my friend Ashley in tears, completely defeated.

She listened, then gently said something I'll never forget:

"I think of my kids like a bottle of soda."

Throughout the school day, that bottle gets shaken. Bumped. Rolled around. They hold it together in class, but that pressure builds. Then, the moment they walk through the door—their safe space—the cap comes off. And everything explodes.

The fizz. The mess. The sticky emotions… all over you.

And honestly? That's how it's supposed to be.

You are their safe space.

The place where they can fall apart.

The person who will love them in the middle of their meltdowns.

Yes, it's messy. Yes, it's exhausting. But Mama, it's also sacred.

Some days aren't about filling your cup—they're about gently cleaning up that shaken bottle, wiping up the mess, and helping your child feel seen, safe, and loved.

And when we do that, something beautiful happens. Their cup starts to refill… and somehow, yours does too.

We're going to mess up.

We'll lose our temper.

We'll raise our voices.

So will they.

But if we keep showing up with love, grace, and forgiveness—just like our Heavenly Father does for us—these hard moments will shape our homes into havens and our children into hearts that know how to handle the messiness of life with grace.

You're not alone. You're not failing. You're raising tiny humans who are still learning—and you're doing it with courage and love, one dinner at a time.

Today's Prayer

Father,

You see me here—in the middle of the chaos, the crumbs on the floor, the noise bouncing off the walls, and the tears I try to blink away at the dinner table.

Lord, I love these children You've given me more than words can say. I miss them when they're away, and I long for connection when they return. But sometimes, the weight of unmet expectations and unspoken hopes leaves me feeling discouraged. I wanted peace… and got spilled milk. I wanted laughter… and got bickering. I wanted connection… and got silence.

And still, You remind me—I am their safe place.

Help me remember that the challenging behavior often hides deeper needs. That their meltdown might really be a cry for love. That their short answers aren't rejection, but exhaustion. And that You, in Your great mercy, entrusted me with the sacred work of loving them through it all.

When I feel worn thin, remind me that You never run out of patience.

When I snap or speak too harshly, help me humble myself, ask for forgiveness, and start again.

When the table feels more like a battleground than a place of peace, help me remember that grace can still be served alongside the food.

Lord, fill my heart with compassion—even when I'm tired. Fill my mouth with gentleness—even when I feel frustrated. And fill our home with reminders of Your presence—even in the mess.

Thank You for giving me the honor of being their mama.

Thank You for being my Safe Place, just as You've called me to be theirs.

In Jesus' name,

Amen.

2 Corinthians 13:14

The grace of the Lord Jesus Christ, and the love of God, and the communion of the Holy Spirit be with you all. Amen.

Psalm 103:8

The Lord is compassionate and gracious, slow to anger, abounding in love.

Day 5

Worthy

It's a question I've asked myself more times than I can count:

Am I still worthy, even though I fail every single day?

I lose my temper.

I say things I shouldn't.

I think things I shouldn't.

I don't pray enough.

I don't read my Bible enough.

And most days, I don't feel like I'm enough.

If you've ever whispered those same words or felt the weight of that guilt pressing on your heart, please know—you're not alone.

But more importantly, God is not surprised by your weakness. He's not sitting on a throne waiting for you to finally "get it right." He's a loving Father who gently picks us up when we fall and walks with us as we try again.

He doesn't expect perfection.

What He desires is a willing heart—one that's honest about its shortcomings, one that turns back to Him over and over again.

So stop trying to be the perfect mom.

The perfect wife.

The perfect daughter, friend, homemaker.

Perfection was never the goal—progress is.

Each day, just aim to be a little more patient, a little more kind, a little more like Jesus than you were the day before.

There has only ever been one perfect person—and we nailed Him to the cross.

And if we would take even a moment each day to reflect on His sacrifice, to remember what He endured for us—the lashes, the mockery, the weight of our sin—it would realign our hearts in ways that no checklist ever could.

I get it, Mama. Life is loud and full. With kids, sports, school, birthday parties, church events—it's a constant cycle. And sometimes we're just bodies in a pew, numb and going through the motions.

But when we finally slow down enough to breathe, to really see Him—we also start to see where we've drifted. And in that moment, we get the chance to return.

Here's what I've learned: our faith isn't a diet.

It's not something we "start fresh" on Monday.

It's not something to push off until tomorrow.

It's a moment-by-moment decision.

So don't wait.

Don't tell yourself you'll open your Bible tomorrow.

Do it today.

Right now.

Even if it's just one verse, one prayer, one quiet cry to the Father who sees you.

He offers grace freely—but that grace was never meant to be taken lightly. We receive it best when we live each day striving to walk in step with Him, even if we stumble along the way.

You are worthy—not because you are perfect, but because He is.

And He chose you.

Today's Prayer

Heavenly Father,

You see me in the quiet places—the moments where I feel like I'm failing, where guilt whispers that I'll never be enough. And yet, You stay. You love. You call me worthy, not because of what I do, but because of who You are.

Lord, I lay down the weight of perfection. I surrender the need to have it all together. Remind me that Your grace is not earned through my performance but received through faith. Help me to return to You daily, not out of duty, but out of love.

When I lose my temper, help me choose patience.
When I speak harshly, help me offer an apology.
When I feel too busy, draw me back to Your Word—even if only for a moment.

Thank You for choosing me to be their mama—for trusting me with these little souls. Strengthen me for the work You've called me to do. And when I fall short, remind me that You never do.

I want to walk closely with You, Lord. Not perfectly—but faithfully.

In Jesus' name,

Amen.

2 Corinthians 12:9

But he said to me, "My grace is sufficient for you, for my power is made perfect in weakness." Therefore I will boast all the more gladly about my weaknesses, so that Christ's power may rest on me.

Lamentations 3:22–23

The steadfast love of the Lord never ceases; his mercies never come to an end; they are new every morning; great is your faithfulness.

Day 6

Spiritual Warfare

Let me tell you something real: if you're making an effort to go to worship, expect resistance. Because we have a very real enemy—and he hates seeing families walking through those church building doors.

The devil doesn't wait until the invitation song to start working—he's stirring up chaos before your feet even hit the floor.

First, the kids won't wake up.

Then they do get up, but someone spills milk or gets toothpaste on their Sunday shirt.

You can't find matching shoes, let alone a coat, and you're carrying a crying child to the car with a diaper bag slung over one shoulder and your coffee left forgotten on the counter.

You're halfway to worship before realizing you forgot your Bible… and your purse. You pull into the parking lot right as the service starts, already mentally and emotionally drained.

And still, you go in.

IMPERFECTLY DEVOTED

You wrangle the little ones into the pew, hoping to soak up just a moment of peace. But before the first song ends, someone needs to use the potty. Then it's a broken crayon, a snack that's suddenly disgusting, and the realization that this coloring book is apparently offensive now.

You feel the tears sting your eyes as you close them for the final prayer. "Why did I even come?" you wonder. "All I did today was fill space on a pew."

But oh Mama—you did so much more than that.

You showed up.

You fought the battle before the battle even began.

And whether you realize it or not, you walked into that building wearing the full armor of God.

When you got those babies out of bed and dressed…

When you fed them, packed the bag, and buckled them in…

When you whispered prayers while brushing hair and smoothing tears…

You were going to war—not against your children, but for them.

And don't miss this: that armor you're wearing? It's not just protecting you—it's guarding them. Every time you choose worship over weariness, you are planting seeds. Every time you bring them into the Lord's house, you are setting a foundation that eternity is built on.

Yes, it feels like chaos.

Yes, it looks messy.

But that's what the battlefield looks like.

Don't be discouraged when worship feels hard. It's hard because it matters. The enemy knows the power of a praying, present mama, and he'll do anything to keep you from showing up.

So tomorrow morning, before your feet even hit the floor—put on the full armor of God.

And Mama, go to battle for those beautiful babies of yours.

Today's Prayer

Heavenly Father,

You see me in the chaos—the spilled milk, the mismatched shoes, the tantrums, the tears. You see me when I feel like I'm failing just trying to get us all out the door and to worship. Thank You for seeing the unseen work, the battles fought behind the scenes, and the love poured out in the smallest, hardest moments.

Lord, I confess, some days I wonder if it's even worth it. But You remind me that every step toward You, no matter how messy or loud, is sacred. Help me remember that bringing my children to Your house is not just a routine—it's a mission. A holy calling.

Give me the strength to keep showing up. Not perfectly, but faithfully.

Clothe me in Your armor. Guard my heart from discouragement and my mind from the lies that say I'm not doing enough.

Help me fight—not against my children, but for them. Let my worship be louder than my weariness, and my faith stronger than my frustration.

Thank You for entrusting me with these little souls. Let every moment spent pointing them to You be multiplied for Your glory. And remind me, even on the hardest mornings, that You

are with me.
You are for me.
And You are proud of me for showing up.

In Jesus' name,

Amen.

Ephesians 6:11

Put on the whole armor of God, that you may be able to stand
against the wiles of the devil.

Galatians 6:9

Let us not become weary in doing good, for at the proper time
we will reap a harvest if we do not give up.

Day 7

Not Enough

The older our children get, the more they test our limits. They push back, talk back, and question everything. For many of us, this is one of the hardest parts of motherhood—the defiance, the attitude, the feeling that no matter how much we give, it's never enough. We pour out our time, energy, and love... and in return, we get slammed doors, eye rolls, or angry words.

It hurts. Deeply.

But when we step back and really reflect, we realize—we've done the same thing to our Heavenly Father. Over and over again.

We want to believe our sin is somehow less offensive. "I'm not a murderer, I'm not stealing..." But Scripture reminds us that sin is sin. Whether it's gossip, bitterness, or pride, it still separates us from God. And still, He forgives us. Still, He loves us. Still, He welcomes us back every time we repent and turn to Him.

So when our kids are in the heat of the moment—when they're yelling, sulking, or saying things they don't even fully understand or mean—we have to remember: they're still learning. They're figuring out how to handle emotions, how to express themselves, how to grow into who they're meant to be. And just like us, they will stumble many, many times.

But we get to be a reflection of God's love to them. That means offering grace, even when they don't "deserve" it. It means discipline, correction with compassion, and forgiveness without strings attached.

We won't always get it right. We'll lose our tempers. We'll say things we shouldn't. But the goal isn't perfection—it's progress. And the beautiful thing? God gave us a guide. His Word is full of truth and instruction on how to parent, how to love, and how to forgive.

We're not parenting alone. We're parenting with the Holy Spirit as our helper, Jesus as our example, and God as our strength.

So on the hard days—when your heart is bruised from your child's words, when nothing you do seems to reach them— remember how the Father loves you. With patience. With compassion. With mercy that never runs out.

Let's offer that same love to our children, again and again. Because that's what changes hearts.

Today's Prayer

Lord,

Some days my heart feels heavy from the weight of motherhood—especially when the ones I love the most push back the hardest. When my child slams a door, rolls their eyes, or speaks with anger, it cuts deep. I try so hard to pour out love, wisdom, and grace… but it doesn't always feel like it's enough.

In those moments, remind me of how I've treated You, Lord— and how You've never turned away from me. You've shown me mercy when I least deserved it. You've corrected me with love and welcomed me back every time I strayed.

Help me reflect that same love to my children.

Fill me with patience when I want to react.
Give me gentleness when I feel like yelling.
Remind me that their defiance is not the end of the story—it's just part of their growing. And You are growing me too.

Guide me through Your Word. Strengthen me with Your Spirit. And teach me how to discipline in love, correct in grace, and always lead my children back to You.

Thank You for being my perfect example of parenthood. Help me walk in Your footsteps, even when the road is hard.

In Jesus' name,

Amen.

Psalm 103:13

Just as a father has compassion on his children, so the Lord has compassion on those who fear Him.

Ephesians 4:32

Be kind to one another, tenderhearted, forgiving one another, as God in Christ forgave you.

Day 8

In the Midst

You are in the thick of it.
Not just the daily chaos—but the soul-deep kind of pain.
The kind that makes you stare at the ceiling at 3 a.m., eyes
burning, tears falling silently beside a sleeping baby or into a
cold pillow.

Maybe it's the fog of postpartum depression—the guilt that
comes with not feeling like yourself, or worse, not feeling
anything at all.
Maybe it's the ache of loss—a parent, a friend, a child—leaving
behind a hole no words can fill.
Maybe it's a health diagnosis, yours or your child's, and you're
carrying the weight of it silently because you're the "strong
one."
Maybe it's your marriage—cold, distant, angry—and you're
exhausted from trying to fix what feels unfixable.

You feel like you're drowning.
You've prayed for rescue. For peace. For relief.
And still, the waters rise.

You wonder: *Where is God in all this?*
Has He forgotten me? Has He left me here to suffer alone?

But He hasn't.
And He never will.

Let's look at Hagar.

She wasn't the "main" wife. She wasn't the center of the
promise. She was a servant, a foreigner, a mother with nowhere
to go and no one to fight for her.
After being mistreated and cast out by people who should have
cared for her, she found herself alone in the wilderness, with
her young son—out of food, out of water, out of hope.

Can you imagine the pain of that moment?
Your child crying from hunger and thirst.
You trying to stay strong, but breaking inside.
Finally setting him down under a bush and walking away
because you *can't bear to watch him die.*

That's how far gone Hagar felt.
That's how real her suffering was.

And then—God showed up.

Not with thunder. Not with lightning.
But with presence.
With provision.
With *hope.*

He called her by name and said, *"What troubles you, Hagar?
Do not be afraid."*

Then He opened her eyes and showed her a well of water right in front of her.

He didn't remove her from the wilderness.
He met her in it.

And He'll do the same for you.

Because He is the God who sees you.
Even when no one else does.
You are not weak for struggling. You are brave for staying in the fight.
You are not less spiritual for asking "Why?"
You are human.
And your Father welcomes even your rawest, realest cries.

He didn't shame Hagar for feeling hopeless.
He showed her where the well was.
He gave her what she needed to keep going.
And He will do the same for you.

Today's Prayer

Father,

You see me.
In the stillness of the night when the tears won't stop…

In the heaviness that sits on my chest when I wake up…
In the chaos I'm barely holding together…
You see it all.

Thank You for being the God who doesn't wait for me to be
strong—You come near when I'm weak.
You don't shame me for my sorrow. You hold me in it.
You didn't abandon Hagar in the wilderness, and You won't
abandon me here either.

Lord, I need You to be my anchor.
When the waves come crashing—when it feels like the ground
is crumbling beneath me—steady me.
Open my eyes to see the well of grace and strength You've
already placed near me.
Help me recognize Your presence, even when the pain doesn't
lift.

Remind me that I'm not forgotten.
Not forsaken.
Not invisible.

You are Emmanuel—God with me.
Not just when things are good, but especially when they are
not.

Today, I choose to hold on to You, not because I feel strong,
but because I know You are.
Even in the thick of it, I trust that You are working, providing,
and holding me together.

In Jesus' name,

Amen.

Genesis 16:13

She gave this name to the Lord who spoke to her: "You are the God who sees me," for she said, "I have now seen the One who sees me."

Psalm 34:18

The Lord is near to the brokenhearted and saves the crushed in spirit.

Day 9

Where Did I Go Wrong?

Mama, today might feel heavy.

The kids are acting out, getting in trouble at school, pushing
every limit at home—and your heart aches because you know
you've poured truth, grace, and guidance into them. You've
read the Scriptures with them, prayed over them while they
slept, spoken life into their hearts.
So why is this happening?

Take a deep breath.

You are not failing.
This is a moment—not the full story.
Children wrestle with right and wrong because they're human.
They test boundaries because they're learning. Even when they
know the truth, sometimes they need to experience the
consequences to truly understand.

Look at the story of the prodigal son (Luke 15:11–32).
The father didn't chase him when he demanded his inheritance
and left home. He let him go, with heartbreak, trusting that the
lessons planted in his heart would eventually draw him back.
And when they did, the father didn't meet him with shame—he
ran to him with open arms and celebrated his return.

IMPERFECTLY DEVOTED

That's how God parents us.
With steadfast love, unshaken grace, and the long view in mind.

Your kids will make mistakes. They may stray from the values
you've instilled. But you are still doing holy, eternal work. You
are planting seeds. And even if the soil seems dry today, God is
the one who waters, grows, and redeems.

Remember—God doesn't require perfection from your
parenting. He invites you to lean on Him.
Let His grace fill the gap between your exhaustion and their
transformation.

You were chosen for this sacred role. Not because it's easy, but
because He equips you through His Spirit. And His Word never
returns void—even when it feels like your kids aren't listening.

Take heart, Mama. You are not alone. Many of us sit with the
same aching questions:
"Where did I go wrong?"
"Why aren't they listening?"

But maybe it's not about doing everything perfectly… maybe
it's about showing up faithfully.
Again and again.
Just like your Father does for you.

BETHANY CLOYD

Today's Prayer

Father,

This calling feels so heavy today. I'm tired. I'm discouraged.
And I'm wondering if I've done something wrong—because
my child's choices are breaking my heart.

Remind me that I am not the Savior—You are.
You love my children more than I ever could.
You see what I can't. You know what I don't.
And You are working, even when I can't see the results.

Help me release control and trust You with the process.
When I'm tempted to give up, give me strength.
When I'm tempted to lash out, give me grace.
When I feel like I've failed, remind me that You parent through
me, even in my weakness.

I place my child—Your child—back into Your hands today.

Thank You for never giving up on me, and for teaching me how
to love like You.

In Jesus' name,

Amen.

2 Thessalonians 3:13

And as for you, brothers and sisters, never tire of doing what is good.

Proverbs 22:6

Train up a child in the way he should go; even when he is old he will not depart from it.

Day 10

God First

We've all heard it — "Put God first!" It's a phrase that's been preached from pulpits and printed on mugs, but if we're being honest... it's easier said than done. Especially for moms. Especially when you're exhausted, pulled in ten different directions, and always giving yourself away to meet the needs of your family.

You wake up early, but not always by choice — it's usually because someone's crying or climbing into your bed, hungry or needing something. In that moment, are we supposed to say, "Hold on, baby, I need to put God first"? No, of course not. You scoop them up, feed them, kiss their cheeks, and love them with your whole heart.

So then what does putting God first really mean in the thick of motherhood?

It means inviting Him into your everything — even the messy, loud, unpredictable parts of your day. Putting God first isn't about a rigid checklist of quiet time, perfect Bible reading, or ideal moments of prayer. It's about living a life built on His presence, His Word, and His grace.

It means whispering a prayer while washing dishes.

IMPERFECTLY DEVOTED

It means turning up worship music while folding laundry.

It means speaking life over your children even when your patience is wearing thin.

It means choosing to respond with grace instead of frustration.

It means teaching your kids to pray — and letting them see you pray too.

Putting God first is making Him the foundation, not just an appointment on your schedule. When He's the foundation of your home, every decision, every moment, every conversation has His fingerprints on it.

It's more than Sunday morning. It's being involved in the body of Christ — not just attending worship, but being the church. It's serving others, teaching your children, and showing them that faith isn't something we do... it's who we are.

It's choosing truth over trends. Maybe that means skipping the newest Netflix series and turning on a podcast that feeds your spirit instead. Maybe it means tuning your car radio to songs that uplift and remind you of God's promises on a hard day.

It's gathering your family around the Word, even if it's five minutes before bedtime or a verse taped to the fridge. It's praying over scraped knees and big emotions, over school days and hard conversations. It's creating a home where Jesus isn't just mentioned—He's central.

Mama, don't be discouraged if "God first" doesn't always look picture-perfect. He sees your heart. He honors your desire to raise your family in faith. He knows your days are full, and He's not asking for perfection—He's asking for your presence.

Build your life on Him, and He will be first. In your home. In your parenting. In your heart.

Today's Prayer

Heavenly Father,

You see me.
You see the dishes piled high, the toys scattered, the endless needs and constant interruptions.
You see the way I try to stretch myself for everyone, even when I feel like I have nothing left to give.

And in the middle of this mess—You still invite me to put You first.
Not through perfection. Not through performance.
But through presence. Through quiet surrender. Through walking with You moment by moment.

So Lord, help me today.

Help me to invite You into the ordinary.
Let my hands become holy as they serve my family.
Let my words be filled with Your gentleness, even when my patience runs thin.
Let my heart remain soft toward You, even when I feel worn and weary.

Remind me that putting You first isn't about a checklist—it's about a relationship.
It's about anchoring every part of my life in You.
Even the diaper changes, the carpool lanes, the midnight wake-ups, and morning chaos.

Be the foundation of my home, God.
Let Your Word guide my parenting, Your Spirit calm my storms, and Your presence fill every room of this house.

When I feel like I'm not doing enough, remind me that You are more than enough.
When I fall short, remind me that Your grace still stands.
And when I feel invisible in the noise of motherhood, remind me that You see me—and You delight in me.

I give You my day.
I give You my family.
I give You my heart.

Be first in all of it, Jesus.
I want to build this life on You.

In Jesus' name,

Amen.

Mathew 6:33

But seek first the kingdom of God and His righteousness, and all these things will be added to you.

Psalm 127:1

Unless the Lord builds the house, those who build it labor in vain.

Day 11

Just Mom

You've heard it before, maybe in different forms:

"Oh, you don't work?"

"So you're just a mom?"

"Don't you get bored being home all day?"

And maybe, on hard days, you've even asked yourself the same questions:

Is this enough?

Am I wasting my potential?

Should I be doing more?

But let me remind you of something sacred—something powerful and true:

You are not just a mom.

You are a disciple-maker, a heart-shaper, a warrior on your knees for your children's souls.

You're not babysitting. You're building foundations.

You're not passing time. You're planting eternity.

You're not behind. You're exactly where God placed you, doing eternal, kingdom-shifting work.

The world may not clap for diaper changes, dishes, and reading Bible stories before nap time. But God sees. And what you're doing matters more than anything this world could ever validate with titles or paychecks.

Yes, it's hard.

Yes, it's repetitive.

Yes, it's quiet and often unseen.

But it's holy.

You are the first voice your children hear each day. The one who gets to whisper truth, model grace, and live out the love of Jesus in front of them daily. You are shaping souls—not just keeping kids alive, but raising children to know, love, and follow Christ.

IMPERFECTLY DEVOTED

This world doesn't need more influencers. It needs more mothers who influence their homes for Jesus.

So the next time someone says, "Oh, you're just a mom?"—you lift your head and smile, because you know better.

You're the gatekeeper of your home.

You're standing in the gap.

You're preparing your children for eternity, not just society.

And Mama, you only have a window—a few short years to plant what will last forever.

Don't waste time wishing for another season.

Don't look at your life and think it's too small.

It's not.

In fact, it will be the greatest work you ever do.

Today's Prayer

Father,

Thank You for calling me to this holy work of motherhood.

Even when it feels ordinary, help me see the extraordinary value in what I'm doing.

Remind me daily that I'm not just a mom—I am shaping eternity and raising the church of tomorrow.

Give me strength when I feel tired, joy when I feel overlooked, and purpose when the days feel long.

Help me raise these precious children to know You deeply and love You fiercely by seeing it reflecting so strongly out of me.

And when doubts whisper that I'm not enough, drown them out with Your truth:

That I am chosen, equipped, and more than enough—because You are enough in me.

In Jesus' name,

Amen.

2 Chronicles 15:7

But as for you, be strong and do not give up, for your work will be rewarded.

Colossians 3:22

Whatever you do, work heartily, as for the Lord and not for men.

Day 12

Slow Down

You hear the thundering footsteps. The laughter turns to squeals, the energy rises, and you pause whatever you're doing because you know what's coming.

"Slow down," you say.

"Someone's going to get hurt," you warn.

But they don't listen.

And just moments later, it happens — the crash, the cry, the consequence.

You scoop them up, soothe their tears, and help them feel safe again. You knew this was going to happen — not because you're mean or trying to ruin their fun, but because you love them. You wanted to protect them.

Sound familiar?

Sometimes, I wonder if that's exactly how God feels about us.

He gives us gentle nudges.

He places caution in our hearts.

He sends His Word to guide us and His Spirit to convict us.

And yet… we rush ahead.

We ignore the signs.

We choose our own way — until we find ourselves crying in the aftermath, whispering through tears, "Lord, help me." and "I'm sorry I didn't listen."

But here's the beauty:

Just like we scoop up our hurting child, God is quick to scoop us up, too.

He doesn't say, "I told you so."

He says, "Come to Me."

He's not watching us from a distance waiting for us to fall—He's with us every step, every stumble, every wrong turn. And when we come back to Him, broken and humbled, He meets us with mercy.

Mama, just like your children need your guidance, you need His.

Don't ignore the warnings He gives.

Don't brush off the conviction in your spirit.

Listen when He says slow down.

Trust when He asks you to wait.

Obey when He says no—even when it doesn't make sense to you.

He sees the whole picture. He loves you too much not to warn you.

Today's Prayer

Father God,

Thank You for loving me enough to warn me.
Thank You for the gentle nudges, the quiet whispers, the uncomfortable stirrings in my spirit that are meant to protect—not punish.
You are not a distant God standing by with judgment.
You are a present and loving Father who sees the whole road ahead, and longs to keep me from unnecessary pain.

IMPERFECTLY DEVOTED

Lord, I confess—
Too often I've rushed ahead.
I've ignored Your voice, convinced I knew better.
I've dismissed Your warnings, only to find myself hurting and asking why.

But even then—You never turned away.
You scooped me up like a child, soothed my aching heart, and reminded me that Your love never left.
Not for a second.

So today, help me slow down.
Help me listen.
Help me trust that Your "no" is not rejection, but protection.
That Your pauses are not punishment, but preparation.

Give me discernment when I feel conflicted.
Give me peace when I'm tempted to push past Your guidance.
Give me humility to admit when I'm wrong, and the courage to obey even when it's hard.

You are the God who sees the crash before it happens.
Who calls out with love, not to ruin our joy—but to preserve it.

So let me be a daughter who listens.
Let me walk closely with You.
Let my children see in me a heart that responds quickly to Your voice—so they may learn to follow You too.

Thank You for always picking me up, dusting me off, and leading me forward.

I trust You, Father.

In Jesus' name,

Amen.

Galatians 6:9

Let us not grow weary in doing good, for at the proper time we will reap a harvest if we do not give up.

Psalm 103:8

The Lord is compassionate and gracious, slow to anger, abounding in love.

Day 13

A Proverbs 31 Woman

Let's be real, Mama.
Reading Proverbs 31 can sometimes feel less like a goal and more like a guilt trip.

This woman is up before dawn, runs a household like a CEO, invests in real estate, clothes her family in scarlet, speaks wisdom, and still has energy to laugh at the future. She's praised by her children and adored by her husband.

Meanwhile…
You're running on 3 hours of sleep, reheating your coffee for the third time, trying to remember if you switched the laundry, and silently praying your toddler doesn't find the permanent markers again.

You love God. You love your family.
But the Proverbs 31 woman?
She sounds unreachable.

But here's the truth the enemy *doesn't* want you to remember:

The Proverbs 31 woman wasn't created to *shame you*—she was meant to inspire you.

This passage wasn't given as a list of impossible standards.
It's a portrait—a collection of seasons and traits cultivated over
time, not overnight.

She didn't wake up one day and magically become all those
things.

She became that woman because she feared the Lord, not
before she did.

You're not failing because your mornings aren't quiet and holy.
You're not less spiritual because your Bible time looks more
like sticky notes and whispered prayers than journals and
commentaries.

You're in the thick of it.
And God sees that.

He's not asking you to become her by tomorrow.
He's asking you to let Him shape you—one obedient step at a
time.

Choosing patience over anger.
Kindness over sarcasm.
Worship instead of worry.
These are the seeds that grow into the woman described in
Proverbs 31.

Don't despise your season—it's where your strength is being
built.

You're already more like her than you think. Because like her, you show up, tired but willing.
You serve.
You pray.
You give.
You try again tomorrow.

That's kingdom work.
That's Proverbs 31 in real time.

Today's Prayer

Lord,

Thank You for showing us what is possible through the Proverbs 31 woman—not to burden us, but to inspire us. Help me to be inspired each time I read it.

On the days I feel like I fall short, remind me that You are shaping me, even in my weakness. Help me to grow in strength, wisdom, and grace—not through my own effort, but by leaning on You. Let me be clothed in dignity, speak life, and serve my family with joy. I invite You into my motherhood, my routine, my heart.

Thank You for the honor of becoming who You created me to be.

In Jesus' name,

Amen.

Proverbs 31:30

Charm is deceptive, and beauty is fleeting; but a woman who fears the Lord is to be praised.

Philippians 1:6

Being confident of this, that He who began a good work in you will carry it on to completion until the day of Christ Jesus;

Day 14

Motherhood

Mama, it's easy to feel unseen in your motherhood.

The world doesn't always applaud the unseen sacrifices, the early mornings and late nights, the meals cooked, the tears wiped, the prayers whispered over sleeping heads. You don't get performance reviews. No one tracks your "promotion." And there are no trophies for folding the fiftieth load of laundry this week.

But the Lord sees you.
 And He calls this holy work.

Motherhood is a sacred calling—not because it's glamorous, but because it's Christlike.

Every diaper changed, every tantrum navigated, every sacrifice made for your children is a quiet echo of the cross. Jesus laid His life down in love, and you do the same every single day— not with grand speeches or dramatic gestures, but in the daily dying to self so your children can flourish.

That's holy.
That's kingdom work.
And yes—that's discipleship.

You are doing what Jesus modeled:

Teaching truth through your words and actions.
Washing little feet and little hearts.
Serving in unseen, humble ways.
Loving when it costs everything.

Whether you're a stay-at-home mom or clock in at a job each day, your presence matters. Your faithfulness matters. The world may not give you a platform, but God has given you something even greater—souls to shepherd.

Every moment with your child is a moment to plant seeds of eternity.
And even if those seeds don't sprout right away, they will take root.

Don't let the noise of culture confuse the mission.
God didn't call you to chase success—He called you to raise disciples.
And He chose you for this assignment on purpose.

You're not just raising children.
You're building the kingdom of God—one bedtime prayer, one scraped knee, one gospel conversation at a time.

Today's Prayer

Heavenly Father,

Thank You for entrusting me with the gift of motherhood. Some days it feels heavy, too holy for someone as tired and imperfect as me. Yet You chose me. You placed these little lives in my hands—not because I have it all together, but because You are the One who holds all things together.

Lord, remind me that the unseen work I do matters to You. When I'm folding laundry again, when I'm up at 3 a.m. with a sick child, when I'm trying to stretch the grocery budget or calm the chaos in the car—let me remember that You are right here with me. You don't overlook my exhaustion or dismiss my small sacrifices. You call this sacred.

Teach me to love like You love—patiently, sacrificially, and without keeping score. Help me to speak words of life into my children, even when I feel drained. When I want to hide or give up, be the strength that keeps me going. When I feel like I'm failing, remind me that You are the grace that covers my gaps.

Help me resist the lies of this world that tell me I'm not doing enough, or that my work isn't valuable. Let me see the eternal impact of the daily, ordinary moments. Give me the wisdom to train up my children in Your truth and the humility to apologize when I fall short. Let my kids see a mom who is dependent on You—not perfect, but present. Not flawless, but faithful.

Jesus, You laid down Your life in love—and I want to walk in Your footsteps every day I mother. Help me to live with an eternal perspective, to find joy in the mundane, and to trust that the seeds I plant today will bear fruit in Your time.

Cover my children with Your protection. Call their hearts to You early and keep them close. May our home be a place where Your name is lifted high and Your peace reigns.

Thank You for walking with me in this calling.
I surrender my motherhood to You again today.

In Jesus' name,

Amen.

Colossians 3:23-24

Whatever you do, work at it with all your heart, as working for the Lord, not for human masters, since you know that you will receive an inheritance from the Lord as a reward. It is the Lord Christ you are serving

Psalm 127:3

Children are a gift from the Lord; they are a reward from Him.

Day 15

Parenting with Christ

Mama, have you ever laid in bed at night and worried yourself sick about your child's future?
What if they walk away from the faith?
What if they get in with the wrong crowd?
What if they never change that attitude or struggle?

That weight you're carrying? You were never meant to carry it alone.

When we parent *without* God—when we operate in our own strength, fueled by fear and the pressure to control—it leads to exhaustion, anxiety, and often, frustration with our kids.
But when we partner *with* Christ, something beautiful happens: peace enters the chaos, grace enters the discipline, and hope anchors the unknown.

We were never meant to be the Savior in our child's life. That role belongs to Jesus.

Of course we should teach them, guide them, correct them—but we cannot change their hearts. Only God can do that. We plant the seeds, we water with prayer and consistency, but He brings the growth.

We see this reflected in Hannah's story in 1 Samuel 1. She desperately wanted a child, and when God gave her Samuel, she *gave him back to the Lord.* She recognized that her job wasn't to cling tightly in fear, but to steward her child in trust—believing God could care for him far better than she ever could.

Jesus also reminds us in John 15:5, "Apart from me you can do nothing." That includes parenting.
But with Him?
With Him, you can train up your children in love and truth, not fear and control.
With Him, you can rest knowing that even when you fall short (and you will), His grace covers you and your kids.
With Him, you can let go of the illusion that it's all on you—and embrace the freedom that comes from walking this journey in partnership with the Creator of your children.

Let today be the day you stop white-knuckling motherhood.
Let go.
Give your children back to God.
He loves them even more than you do—and He's not leaving you to raise them alone.

Today's Prayer

Father,

Thank You for the precious gift of motherhood. It is holy and
beautiful—but it is also heavy. And I confess that so often, I try
to carry it all myself. I try to be everything my children need. I
try to control, fix, or fearfully predict every outcome.
Forgive me for forgetting that You are their Creator, their
Savior, and their Provider.

Teach me how to parent with You—not for You.
Help me to surrender my control and place my children into
Your loving, capable hands.
Give me wisdom when I don't know what to say.
Give me peace when outcomes feel uncertain.
Give me grace when I mess up.
And help me rest, knowing You are always working behind the
scenes—shaping, guiding, and loving my children even more
than I ever could.

In Jesus' name,

Amen.

Proverbs 3:5-6

Trust in the Lord with all your heart and lean not on your own understanding; in all your ways submit to Him, and He will make your paths straight.

Psalm 37:5

Commit your way to the Lord; trust in Him and He will do this.

Day 16

Unspoken Truths

Motherhood has a way of shining a light on all the parts of us we wish would stay hidden.
Impatience. Anger. Control. Fear. Exhaustion. Selfishness.

Before I had children, I thought I was a fairly kind and steady person. But add a sleepless night, a toddler meltdown, and dishes piled in the sink, and suddenly I'm not so steady. I'm short-tempered, easily overwhelmed, and questioning if I'm even cut out for this.

And then there are the times I've pulled away from God—
Not intentionally, but subtly.
One missed quiet time turns into a week.
One rushed prayer becomes silence.
One hard day becomes a season of spiritual dryness just keeping the pew warm.

This is the drifting away that Hebrews 2:1 warns us about.

I know the truth. I know I need Him. But sometimes I feel too far gone to open my Bible.
Too ashamed of the yelling.
Too guilty for the resentment.
Too tired to pray.

And yet… when I finally whisper, "Lord, I'm sorry,"
He's there.

He was never gone.

When I finally open my Bible again, it's not with judgment—
it's with welcome.

When I cry tears of regret over the angry words I spoke to my
kids,
He's not wagging a finger—He's pulling me close.

When I've drifted into numbing out on my phone instead of
leaning into His peace,
He gently invites me to come back.

He is the Father of the prodigal.
He runs *toward* us, not away.

He doesn't wait for us to "clean up" before we return - as long
as our hearts see the wrong they've done and we repent and try
our best to walk in His path of righteousness. We will always
be falling short, but don't focus on that part. Focus on that He
forgives when we move towards Him with a heart on fire for
Him.

Today's Prayer

Father God,

You know my heart.
You've seen my tears, my failures, my silence.
You've watched as I pulled away in the chaos of
motherhood—
not because I don't love You,
but because I've been tired, overwhelmed, and unsure how to
come back.

I confess my impatience.
My sharp words.
My pride when I try to do it all on my own.
I confess the days I've ignored Your voice and chased after
things that don't fill.
Forgive me, Lord.

Thank You for never leaving me,
for being near, even when I wasn't looking for You.
Thank You for the grace that meets me in the mess,
for mercy that doesn't run out,
and for love that welcomes me home every single time.

Help me, Jesus.
To turn to You in the thick of it—
in the laundry piles, the late nights, the meltdowns, the
moments I feel like I've failed.

Draw me back when I drift.
 Soften my heart when it's hardened.
 Renew my desire to seek You again.

Thank You that I don't have to earn my way back into Your
presence.
 You never moved.
 You've been holding space for me all along.

I want to walk with You again.
 Teach me how, even in this busy season of motherhood.
 Help me rest in Your love and walk in Your grace—one
moment, one step at a time.

In Jesus' name,

 Amen.

Joel 2:13

Return to the Lord your God, for He is merciful and compassionate, slow to get angry and filled with unfailing love.

Luke 15:20

But while he was still a long way off, his father saw him and was filled with compassion for him; he ran to his son, threw his arms around him and kissed him.

Day 17

Fit Into Heaven

Let's just be honest—parenting is hard. Some days it feels like the hardest thing you've ever done. You're tired, you're questioned, you're second-guessed (especially by your own kids), and you're constantly swimming upstream in a world that celebrates everything except what you're trying to instill in your home.

Maybe your children think you're the worst mom ever because you don't let them have a phone like "everyone else."

Maybe you have rules in your home that make them feel like outsiders compared to their friends.

Maybe you're exhausted from always being the one who says no when the world is shouting yes.

But mama—please hear this: you are doing holy work.

You are not raising your children to blend in.

You are raising them to stand out.

You are raising them for heaven.

And that means it's going to look different. It's going to feel lonely sometimes—for both you and them. It's going to be hard to hold the line when their eyes are full of tears and all they want is to fit in. But our goal was never to help them fit into the world.

We are called to something higher. Our homes are training grounds—not for popularity, not for worldly success, but for eternity. The boundaries you set now, the truth you speak over them, the prayers you whisper over their sleepy heads, they all matter. More than you can see right now.

We don't just discipline for obedience—we discipline because we're preparing their hearts for the day they'll have to choose right from wrong on their own.

We don't just say no to protect their innocence—we say no to protect their souls.

So let them think your rules are different—because they are. You are pouring out God's truth over them at every opportunity, whether they realize it or not. You are sowing seeds that may not bloom for years, but trust me, they are being planted.

You're not just fighting for a peaceful day—you're fighting for their eternal salvation.

And that battle is so worth it.

One day, the tantrums will fade. The school drop-offs will end. The bickering will be a memory. But their souls? They're forever. One day, they will stand before the Lord, and when He looks at them, I pray He sees the impact of your sacrifice, your consistency, your love, your prayers, and your refusal to give up.

Mama, stay in the fight. Don't back down, even when it's lonely. Don't let the world convince you that you're too strict, too different, or too out of touch. Let your goal be this: that your children don't fit in with the world... because they belong in heaven.

That's what this is all about.

And on the days it feels like too much, lift your eyes. You are not alone in this work. The Lord sees you, equips you, and walks beside you.

Because while we can't take anything from this world into eternity, we can take souls with us. And those precious children in your care are the most important ones of all.

Today's Prayer

Heavenly Father,

Some days I feel so worn down. The world presses in from
every direction, and I feel like I'm swimming upstream—alone,
exhausted, misunderstood. Lord, You see every tear I've cried
behind closed doors, every moment I've questioned if I'm
doing the right thing, every time I've wanted to give in and just
make it easier.

But I don't want easy—I want *eternal.*

So today, I ask for courage. Give me boldness to stand firm
when my children push back, when culture says I'm too strict,
when others don't understand the convictions I hold. Help me to
remember that I'm not parenting for comfort or convenience—
I'm parenting for the Kingdom.

Give me strength, Lord, to say "no" when it would be easier to
say "yes." Give me wisdom to lead my children in truth when
the lies of this world scream louder. Help me to set boundaries
in love, not fear. And when those boundaries bring tears or
anger or loneliness, let my heart rest in Your approval—not the
world's.

Thank You for entrusting me with these souls. What a holy
calling. I don't take it lightly. Forgive me for the days I've tried
to do it all in my own strength—for the moments I've snapped,

doubted, or withdrawn. Thank You for Your endless mercy that picks me back up and puts me back in the fight.

Lord, I lift my children to You. Shape their hearts. Draw them close. Even when they don't understand my choices now, may they one day look back and see You woven through every decision, every correction, every prayer.

Help me raise children who don't fit in with the world— because they were never meant to. May they be a light in the darkness, a reflection of Your truth, and a testimony to Your grace. Let our home be a place where Your presence dwells and where eternity is the goal.

And on the days when I feel unseen, remind me that You see it all. Every sacrifice. Every whispered prayer. Every holy no.

Thank You for walking this road with me, Jesus. I can't do it without You. But with You? I have everything I need.

In Jesus' name,

Amen.

Romans 12:2

Do not conform to the pattern of this world, but be transformed
by the renewing of your mind.

3 John 1:4

I have no greater joy than to hear that my children are walking
in the truth.

Day 18

Bad Dreams

There's something about nighttime that makes worries louder. Maybe it's the quiet, maybe it's the stillness—but for our two youngest boys, bedtime became a battle against fear. Night after night, they'd wake up from bad dreams—scared, crying, and anxious to close their eyes again.

So we started a new routine. Every night before bed, we added a new prayer—what we now call the *Dream Prayer*:

"Lord, protect me. Make me brave. Make me strong. Make me tough. Give me good sleep and no bad dreams."

That simple little prayer began to shift everything. They found peace. They trusted that once we prayed, God was going to take care of it. And you know what? They slept soundly.

That prayer—born out of fear—became a declaration of faith. And those little boys taught me a powerful lesson:

They didn't just *say* the prayer.
They *believed* it.
And then they went to sleep in peace.

How often do we, as adults, do the opposite?
We pray and ask God for help, but then we keep worrying.
We ask Him to carry the burden, but we still hold onto it.

Jesus told us to come to Him with faith like children.

Children trust simply and fully. They don't overthink or
second-guess. When they believe something, they believe it all
the way. That's the kind of faith God is calling us to.

Not because it's childish—but because it's dependent.

Just like our boys found peace when they handed their fears to
God through prayer, we too can rest when we truly release our
worries into His hands.

What burden are you still holding onto today?
What prayer have you prayed but not truly released?

We can't let ourselves be double-minded and unstable as James
1:6-8 speaks of.

Let's build our faith—not by having all the answers, but by
learning to trust like our children do. Let's pray with
expectation, rest in His promises, and walk with the kind of
unshakable belief that He is who He says He is.

Because He is.

And He's listening.

Today's Prayer

Heavenly Father,

You are so good and so kind, and yet so often I forget. I come to You with my prayers, my worries, my burdens—and instead of releasing them, I keep holding onto them, letting them weigh down my heart. Forgive me for the times I've trusted more in my own control than in Your promises. Forgive me for praying while still planning my own backup. I want to trust You fully, Lord.

You've told me to have faith like a child—to believe without doubting, to ask without fear, to rest in the peace that comes from knowing I am held by You. Lord, help me return to that kind of simple, wholehearted trust. The kind that prays and then sleeps peacefully. The kind that believes Your Word without question. The kind that knows You are both mighty and near.

Teach me through the little ones You've placed in my life. I see their trust, their dependence, their open hearts—and I long to mirror that in my walk with You. Remind me that You're not frustrated by my weakness, but You're drawing me closer. When I'm overwhelmed, show me how to pause and pray. When fear creeps in, teach me to speak Your truth aloud. When I'm tempted to worry, lead me back to Your promises.

God, I release my anxious thoughts to You. The things I can't control—the fears about my children, my future, my family, my finances—I give them to You now. Not with fingers still clenched, but with open hands and a surrendered heart. You are trustworthy. You are faithful. You are with me, always.

Thank You for being a God who hears. A God who sees. A God who is never tired of my returning. You welcome me back every time with grace. So here I am again, Lord—learning to trust, to rest, to believe like a child. Strengthen my faith, anchor my heart in You, and help me teach this kind of trust to my children too.

In Jesus' name,

Amen.

Matthew 18:3

Truly I tell you, unless you change and become like little children, you will never enter the kingdom of heaven.

Isaiah 26:3

You will keep in perfect peace those whose minds are steadfast, because they trust in you.

Day 19

Not Enough Credit

You ever have one of *those* days?
 The kind where everyone's on edge, the kids are bickering nonstop, your spouse is short with you, and you feel overwhelmed by a cloud of frustration you can't shake? You've done all the "right" things—read your Bible, said your prayers, kept the peace—but your house still feels like a battlefield.

And maybe that's exactly what it is.

Too often, we look at our struggles and ask God, *"Why are You letting this happen?"* when, in truth, the battle we're experiencing may not be from Him at all—it may be from the one who *hates* what God is building in your home.

We don't give the enemy enough credit. Satan is real, and Scripture tells us clearly that the devil is "a roaring lion, seeking whom he may devour" (1 Peter 5:8). His mission is simple: *"to steal, kill, and destroy"* (John 10:10). That includes stealing your joy, killing your peace, and destroying the unity in your home.

So no, not every bad day is just hormones, tiredness, or coincidence. Sometimes it's spiritual warfare.

But here's the good news: you're not helpless.

God has equipped you with the *armor of God* (Ephesians 6:10–18) to stand firm against the enemy's schemes. You have access to the name of Jesus—the name that makes demons tremble. You have the authority to call out the darkness and invite the light of Christ into your home.

You don't need to fear calling the devil out. In fact, ignoring him only gives him more room to stir things up. When you sense things going sideways—when your family feels attacked, your heart feels burdened, and the atmosphere is tense—pause. Pray. Declare the name of Jesus over your home. Out loud.

Say it even if you feel silly.
Say it even if you're not sure what's going on.
Say it *especially* when you feel under spiritual attack.

You may not always know whether it's a test from God or an attack from the enemy, but either way—God is your refuge. Run to Him, and He will respond. "Resist the devil, and he will flee from you" (James 4:7). "Call upon Me in the day of trouble; I will deliver you" (Psalm 50:15).

Don't be afraid to name the enemy—but don't ever forget who has already won the war.

Today's Prayer

Lord,

There are days where everything feels heavy—like my home is filled with tension and my heart is overwhelmed. On those days, help me remember that there is more going on than what I see. Remind me that we wrestle not against flesh and blood, but against spiritual forces of evil. Open my eyes to recognize the enemy's schemes—and give me boldness to stand in Your truth.

In the name of Jesus, I speak peace over my home. I ask You to cover us in Your protection. Drive out anything not from You—fear, strife, confusion, anxiety. Fill our space with Your Spirit, Your calm, and Your joy. Teach me to war in prayer, to fight with faith, and to trust that no matter what comes against me, You are greater.

I will not give fear the final say.

I will not let the enemy steal what You've given.

I will stand, with You as my refuge.

In Jesus' name,

Amen.

Psalm 34:17

The righteous cry out, and the Lord hears them; He delivers
them from all their troubles.

James 4:7

Submit yourselves, then, to God. Resist the devil, and he will
flee from you.

Day 20

Pink?

You've probably heard the saying: *"Flamingos lose their pink when they become mothers."*
It's often used as a metaphor for moms—how we "lose ourselves" in motherhood and how, one day, we'll "get our pink back."

But what if that's not the goal?
What if we were never meant to return to the same vibrant pink we once were?
What if, instead, God is painting us into something new— something even more radiant?

Because here's the truth: **motherhood changes everything.**
Your body is different.
Your sleep, your priorities, your daily rhythm—it all shifts.
Your heart? Oh, how it *expands.*
Your mind constantly scans for danger, worries, schedules, snacks, school forms, and spiritual needs.
You are not who you used to be—and that's not a bad thing.
It's holy.

We often long to "get back to ourselves." But friend, maybe God doesn't want you to go back.

Because just like new life came from your body, a new life is also being formed inside *you*.

When you became a mother, God didn't ask you to cling to your old identity.
He invited you to grow into a *new one*.

This transformation reminds me of what Scripture says about becoming a new creation in Christ:

> "Therefore, if anyone is in Christ, the new creation
> has come: The old has gone, the new is here!"
> — 2 Corinthians 5:17

We are changed—forever—when we give our lives to Jesus.
We lay down our old ways, our selfish desires, our sin, and we become someone new.
Motherhood mirrors that transformation.
We lay down our comfort, our bodies, our time, and in its place, God gives us something eternal.

Just as baptism represents dying to our old self and being raised into a new life in Christ, motherhood represents a dying to self in the most daily, raw, and sacrificial ways.

You may not wear the same jeans.
You may not have time for the same hobbies.
You may look in the mirror and see someone unrecognizable.

But what you've gained?

A deeper strength.
A fiercer love.
A wider heart.
A holy calling.

So no—you don't need to get your "pink" back.
You need to embrace the new color God is painting you into.

A color that glows with grace.
That shimmers with surrender.
That radiates with the kind of love only a mother—and a
woman anchored in Christ—can carry.

Today's Prayer

Lord,

Thank You for the gift and the calling of motherhood.

Even when I don't recognize the woman in the mirror—when I
feel like I've lost myself in the noise, the mess, the constant
giving—I know You are shaping me into something new and
beautiful.

Help me not to cling to what once was, but to embrace who
You are making me to be. Let me walk in this new identity with

confidence, knowing that every sacrifice, every stretch, every sleepless night is not unnoticed by You.

Strengthen me to see motherhood not as something that's taken from me, but something that's *grown* me—closer to You, deeper in love, stronger in spirit.

I don't need to get my pink back, Lord.

I just want to radiate with the new color You're painting on my life.

Make me more like You—daily, fully, joyfully.

In Jesus' name,

Amen.

Romans 12:1

Therefore, I urge you, brothers and sisters, in view of God's mercy, to offer your bodies as a living sacrifice, holy and pleasing to God—this is your true and proper worship.

Ephesians 4:24

And put on the new self, created after the likeness of God in the true righteousness and holiness.

Day 21

Can't Shake It

You're having a bad day.
 Or maybe it's been a string of them—bad weeks, even a whole
month where the weight just won't lift.

You're tired in a way that sleep doesn't fix.
 You snap when you don't want to.
 You cry over the dishes.
 You forget appointments and question your worth.
 You're stuck in a fog, and no matter how many deep breaths
you take or how many self-help reels you watch—you still feel
lost.

Friend, I see you. And more importantly, God sees you too.

I've been in that place—ashamed to admit how easily I shut
down. I stop praying. I stop reading. I sulk, feel numb, and tell
myself I'll try again tomorrow. But somehow, tomorrow
doesn't come. The heaviness lingers, and I start to believe the
lie that maybe I'm too far gone.

But here's the truth: you are not a lost cause.

This darkness? This fog? It doesn't define you.
And it doesn't scare God.

He's still there.
Still listening.
Still ready.

You don't have to fix yourself before coming to Him.
You just have to come.

When you *pray* again—even through tired tears—your soul
exhales.
When you *read* the Word again—just one verse—it starts to
stir something in you.
And when you *seek* Him, the fog doesn't always disappear
instantly—but you begin to remember who you are and whose
you are.

You're not just a mom. You are a daughter of the King.
And He never grows tired of you needing Him.

Those tiny hands tugging at your pants?
Those loud little voices pushing all your buttons?
They are watching.
And when they see you cry out to God, when they see
you open your Bible, when they hear you speak His name
even in struggle—they learn where to run when *they* feel
stuck too.

So today, don't run away.
 Don't hide.
Don't wait for it to feel easier.
 Start where you are. Right now.

Whisper a prayer. Open the Word. Let the Living Water do
what only He can—*revive what feels dry and empty.*

Mama, you're not alone.
 You're not too far gone.
 You are deeply loved and still held—right in the middle of the
mess.

Today's Prayer

Lord,

 You know my heart. You see the heaviness I carry—the
weariness that no one else understands. I confess that I've
pulled away from You. I've let the weight of life push me into
silence. I've avoided prayer, avoided Your Word, and tried to
do it all on my own. But today, I want to come back.

Even if all I can say is "help," I know You hear.
 Even if all I can manage is one verse, I know it matters.
 Thank You for never leaving, even when I drift. Thank You for
still welcoming me with grace.

Fill me again, Lord. Strengthen my heart.

Remind me of who I am in You—chosen, loved, and never too far gone.

Help me be the mother You've called me to be, not through my own strength but by abiding in Yours.

And let my children see what it means to run to You, even when life is hard.

I trust You with this season, and I ask You to carry me through it—one day at a time.

In Jesus' name,

Amen.

Psalm 34:18

The Lord is close to the brokenhearted and saves
those who are crushed in spirit.

Isaiah 40:29

He gives strength to the weary and increases the
power of the weak.

Day 22

All it Takes is Nothing

Drifting away from God doesn't always start with rebellion.
It doesn't always look like a crisis, a scandal, or a life-altering
sin.

Sometimes, it looks like... nothing.
No prayer.
No time in the Word.
No quiet moments of worship.
No intentional fellowship.

Just busy days.
Endless to-do lists.
A distracted heart.
And before you know it—you've drifted.

That's how spiritual drift happens.
Not with a bang... but with a slow fade.

The busyness of motherhood makes it so easy to drift away if
we aren't careful.

And friend, this is exactly how Satan works best—not always
through obvious destruction, but through quiet distractions.

IMPERFECTLY DEVOTED

He fills your plate until you're too tired to pray.
He fills your schedule until worship feels like a luxury.
He fills your head with lies that say:

> "You're too busy. You'll read tomorrow. God
> understands."

And it's true—God does understand.
But He also desires a relationship with you.
One that's alive, present, and growing.

Drift requires nothing. But devotion requires something.
To stay near to God, you have to *do something.*
Even something small.

A whispered prayer while folding laundry.
A verse taped to your bathroom mirror.
A worship song on your drive to school drop-off.
A few minutes in His Word before bed.

These moments?
They add up.
They *anchor* you.

The truth is, we don't just "fall" away from God…
We fade when we stop fighting for connection.
We drift when we stop pursuing the One who never stops
pursuing us.

You were never meant to do this alone.
That's why He gave us community.
Fellowship.
His Spirit.
His Word.

When your soul starts to feel dry—don't ignore it.
Don't let "nothing" become the very thing that separates you
from the One who loves you most.

Start small.
Start now.
Do something.

Today's Prayer

Lord,

Forgive me for the times I've drifted—not in defiance, but in
distraction. Life gets loud, and I forget how much I need You. I
don't want to do nothing and watch my relationship with You
quietly fade. Help me pay close attention to the state of my
heart. Help me recognize when I've let the urgent things crowd
out what's truly important.

Teach me to fight for connection.
To choose You first.
To draw near—one small moment at a time.

Protect me from the subtle schemes of the enemy who would love to keep me busy, tired, and distant.
Make me alert, make me hungry for Your Word, and fill me again with passion for Your presence.

Even when I feel overwhelmed, remind me that You are not asking for perfection—just pursuit.
I want to stay close to You, Jesus.
Pull me back when I start to drift.
And thank You for always welcoming me when I return.

In Jesus' name,

Amen.

Hebrews 2:1

We must pay the most careful attention, therefore, to what we have heard, so that we do not drift away.

James 4:8

Draw near to God and He will draw near to you.

Day 23

Comparison

Comparison might seem innocent at first—just noticing another mom's tidy home. How does she do it with so many kids running around? Well-behaved kids. Mine can't stop mimicking each other and seem to defy everything I say. Or that flawless postpartum body. She just had a baby and you can't even tell, yet I'm three years postpartum and carrying around 30 pounds I can't seem to lose no matter what I do. The effects of all of this comparison can run deep. It plants seeds of inadequacy, discouragement, and self-doubt. And Mama, that is exactly what the enemy wants.

You've been there before. At the park, the grocery store, or scrolling your phone—seeing another mom who seems to have it all together while your toddler is melting down and your shirt is stained with spit-up. You wonder, *What am I doing wrong? Why can't I look like her, act like her, parent like her?*

And just like that, the joy of your own journey begins to fade.

But let's be real: comparison is not from God.

In fact, Scripture tells us that comparison robs us of peace.

Comparison invites envy, and envy opens the door to all sorts of lies. Lies that say you're not enough. That your motherhood is lacking. That you'll never measure up. But friend, you were never meant to measure yourself by another woman's story. You were created uniquely, called specifically, and gifted perfectly for the children God gave you.

Just like Martha, distracted by the work and frustrated that Mary wasn't "doing enough" (Luke 10:38–42), we too often forget what really matters. Jesus lovingly told Martha that Mary had chosen what was better—to sit at His feet. Not to worry about appearances or keeping up, but to draw near to Him.

And that's what He calls us to do. Not to compare. But to focus. Focus on the good, the grace, the small wins, the faithfulness of God even in the mess.

So the next time you see "that mom" and feel less-than, pause and remember this truth:

> "Each one should test their own actions. Then they
> can take pride in themselves alone, without
> comparing themselves to someone else."
> —Galatians 6:4

You are not called to be *her*.
You are called to be *you*, walking in God's purpose for *your* family.

Let's stop looking sideways. Let's look up.

Today's Prayer

Father,

I confess that I've allowed comparison to steal my joy.
I've looked at other moms and felt like I don't measure
up—physically, spiritually, emotionally.

Forgive me for focusing on what I lack instead of what
You've blessed me with. Help me to see my own journey
as valuable and sacred. Open my eyes to the beauty in my
home, the gifts in my children, and the calling You've
placed on my life. Help me choose gratitude over envy
and contentment over striving.

 Remind me daily that my worth is found in You—not in
how I compare to others. Thank You for walking with me
every step of this motherhood journey.

In Jesus' name,

Amen.

James 3:16

For where envy and selfish ambition exist, there is
disorder and every evil practice.

Proverbs 14:30

A heart at peace gives life to the body, but envy
rots the bones.

Day 24

Confidence

Confidence. It's a word we hear a lot—but rarely feel deep in our bones.

As moms and women, confidence often feels just out of reach. Whether it's how our body looks in the mirror, how we handle the tantrums and chaos of parenting, how we communicate in our marriages, or how we show up in the world—we're quick to second-guess ourselves. We question if we're enough, if we're doing it right, and if we're truly capable.

But friend, there is one place we are called to have unshakable confidence: our faith.

> "So do not throw away your confidence; it will be
> richly rewarded."
> —Hebrews 10:35

This isn't self-confidence rooted in what we can do, but God-confidence rooted in who He is and what He's done.

When we are confident in our salvation—knowing that we have been saved, buried with Him in baptism and raised to a new life—it becomes a lens through which we view every part of our lives. That kind of confidence changes us. It frees us from the pressure of trying to be perfect and instead empowers us to walk in the truth of God's love and purpose for us.

You might not love the way your body looks. But when you remember you were created in His image (Genesis 1:27), your value isn't tied to your pant size—it's tied to your identity as His beloved daughter.

You might feel insecure in your parenting. But when you remember that He equips those He calls (Hebrews 13:21), you can walk forward trusting that He will fill the gaps you can't.

You may carry scars from betrayal or broken relationships. But when your marriage is built on the solid rock of Christ, you both submit to Him first (Ephesians 5:21-25). Trust becomes less about controlling every situation and more about surrendering to the One who holds your future.

True confidence doesn't mean we always feel good about ourselves—but it does mean we know Whose we are and why we stand firm in our faith. When our confidence is rooted in Christ, it overflows into every other area of our life. It transforms our perspective, gives us peace, and reminds us that we are never walking alone.

So today, Mama, let your confidence rest in the One who never fails.

Today's Prayer

Father,

I come to You as a woman who often feels unsure of herself. I doubt my worth, question my abilities, and too easily listen to the lies that say I'm not enough. But Lord, You say I am fearfully and wonderfully made. You say I am chosen, redeemed, and called.

Help me to rest in that truth today. Help me to build my confidence not in what I see in the mirror or how others treat me, but in who You are. May my faith be the solid ground I walk on—secure in the knowledge that You are with me, working in me, and carrying me every step of the way. Let that confidence shine into my motherhood, my relationships, and my daily life. Thank You for being the anchor when I feel adrift.

In Jesus' name,

Amen.

Hebrews 10:35

So do not throw away your confidence; it will be richly rewarded.

Proverbs 3:26

For the Lord will be your confidence and will keep your foot from being caught.

Day 25

Set Apart

Motherhood changes us—and often overnight. One moment, we're just ourselves, and the next, we're someone's whole world. The sleepless nights begin. The days are filled with lullabies, diapers, baby talk, and cartoon theme songs. Spontaneous nights out become memories, replaced by late-night rocking chairs and tiny, milk-drunk smiles. And somehow, in the middle of all the exhaustion and adjustment, our hearts expand in a way we never thought possible. We're changed—and it shows.

The same is true when we become followers of Christ.

No, we don't walk out of the waters of baptism with everything perfectly figured out. But something very real and undeniable happens: our heart has been transformed. There's a stirring in us. A hunger. A desire to live differently because we've encountered the One who gave everything for us.

Just like people can usually tell you're a mom even when your kids aren't with you—the way you carry yourself, the diaper bag in tow, the love in your eyes—the world should also be able to tell you are a child of God.

You begin to make time for prayer and the Word. Church services become sacred and non-negotiable. You crave truth more than trends. Your speech, your habits, your priorities— they begin to reflect the Spirit now dwelling inside of you.

> "You are the light of the world. A city set on a hill cannot be hidden."
> —Matthew 5:14

Mama, this is something to celebrate. This is what it means to be set apart, holy, marked by the grace of God. And the change? It's not something we have to force—it flows from the deep, abiding relationship we now have with Christ.

We no longer blend in—and we shouldn't. The world may not always understand our choices. It may raise eyebrows when we choose worship over worldly pleasures, when we raise our kids in faith, when we say no to what's "normal." But that's the point.

That transformation—the one that begins in your heart—will shape every part of you, just like motherhood does. And even if it feels like the change is happening fast and all at once, don't worry. God is guiding your every step. He doesn't expect perfection—He simply asks for your surrender.

Let the world see your light. Let them notice that there's something different about you. Let your faith be as visible as your mama-heart.

Because when you know the Lord, you can't help but be changed.

Today's Prayer

Heavenly Father,

Thank You for the beautiful transformation You've begun in me. Just as motherhood has reshaped my heart, my mind, and my daily life, so has Your presence reshaped my soul. You have made me new—not perfect, but changed. And in that change, I see Your love and mercy at work.

There are days when I miss who I used to be—when I feel overwhelmed by all that motherhood and faith require of me. But Lord, remind me that I am not called to go back. I am called forward, into the purpose You've created me for. Help me to release the pressure to have it all together, and instead rest in the truth that You are working in me day by day.

Let my faith be visible—not just in what I say, but in how I live. Let others see You in my patience, in my priorities, and even in my struggles. When I feel tempted to blend in with the world, give me the courage to stand out for You. When I feel weary or unseen, remind me that You are always with me, cheering me on and holding me close.

Lord, thank You for the sacred calling of motherhood and for the holy transformation of salvation. Help me to live each day with confidence, grace, and joy, knowing that who I am becoming is all because of You. I surrender my past, my present, and my future to You. Mold me. Use me. Shine through me.

In Jesus' name,

Amen.

Romans 12:2

Do not conform to the pattern of this world, but be transformed by the renewing of your mind.

2 Corinthians 5:17

Therefore, if anyone is in Christ, he is a new creation. The old has passed away; behold, the new has come.

Day 26

Rest

Rest.
 A word that sounds like a luxury to most moms. Because how *do* you rest when someone's always up with a bad dream, teething, or a cough that won't quit? And if the house is actually quiet, your mind won't be. The to-do list screams at you. Or you finally have a moment alone and binge a show or scroll in silence—not because you're lazy, but because your soul is tired. You just need something that doesn't *need* you.

And still, the guilt creeps in.
 "I shouldn't be taking a break."
 "Moms don't get days off."
 "There's too much to do."

But here's the truth:
 You were not created to run on empty. You were not made to constantly pour without being filled.

Even Jesus—our Savior, our perfect example—*rested.*

If Jesus needed rest and stillness to reconnect with the Father and be renewed, how much more do *we* need that?

You are not just doing laundry or cooking dinner or answering endless questions. You are shaping souls. That is *holy work*. But holy work doesn't mean hustle every second. It means obeying the rhythm God created: work and rest.

> "By the seventh day God had finished the work he had been doing; so on the seventh day he rested from all his work."
> — Genesis 2:2

God Himself modeled rest. Not because He was tired—but because He was showing us how to live. Rest is not weakness. It's worship. It's a declaration of trust—saying, "God, I believe You'll take care of what I don't get done today. I believe I don't have to do it all to be worthy."

So Mama, take the nap.
 Ask your husband to take the kids for an hour.
 Go for the walk.
 Light the candle and read the chapter.
 Take the bath.
 Sit in the silence.
 Pray.

You are allowed to rest. In fact, you're *instructed* to.

Let the Lord fill what's empty. He's not looking for the most productive version of you—He's pursuing the most present version of you. One who sits with Him. One who receives His peace. One who understands that burnout is not a badge of honor.

Let today be the day you stop apologizing for needing rest. It's biblical. It's necessary. And it will renew you to love your people well.

Today's Prayer

Father,

You are the Creator of rest, the One who knows our limits and lovingly invites us to slow down. Lord, I confess that I often feel guilty for needing rest, like I have to earn it or prove that I'm doing enough. But You remind me that rest is not laziness—it's obedience. It's trust. It's needed.

Help me to recognize the signs of burnout before they break me. Teach me how to make space for quiet moments with You, even in the middle of the chaos. When I feel like there's too much to do, help me surrender my need for control and choose stillness with You.

Restore my soul, Lord. Help me rest without guilt. Help me see that taking care of myself is part of loving my family well.

Thank You for never asking me to carry more than I can handle without You. I give You my exhaustion, and I receive Your peace.

In Jesus' name,

Amen.

Luke 5:16

But Jesus often withdrew to lonely places and prayed.

Matthew 11:28

Come to me, all you who are weary and burdened, and I will give you rest.

Day 27

Mom Guilt

"I gave them the tablet... again. We've eaten fast food three nights this week. I didn't read them a bedtime story. Did they even brush their teeth today?"

Sound familiar?

Mom guilt is one of the enemy's favorite tools. It sneaks into the most vulnerable cracks in our day and tries to convince us that we're not enough. That we're lazy, failing, behind. That other moms are doing it better. That we've somehow messed up our kids because we chose rest over routine, or survival over perfection.

We carry the weight of every decision. We second-guess every choice. We play comparison games that always leave us feeling defeated. We cry quietly in the bathroom while little fists bang on the door.

And yet — God sees it all.
 And He calls us loved, not lacking.

Friend, guilt is not from God. Conviction leads us to repentance and growth, but guilt rooted in shame? That's a lie meant to rob your joy. Yes, some days we mess up. Some days we get short-tempered, forget appointments, serve frozen waffles for dinner, and give in to the tantrum just to keep peace.

But those things don't define your motherhood.
 What defines your motherhood is *faithfulness* — showing up again, trying again, praying again.

Let's remember that even the most faithful mothers in Scripture were still just human. Hannah wept in desperation before she saw her promise fulfilled. Mary lost Jesus for three whole days. Even Naomi felt like she had nothing left to give and renamed herself "bitter."

But God was still in the story.

And He's still in yours.

When we see another mom with a Pinterest-worthy lunchbox or kids who say "yes ma'am" on command, it's tempting to feel like we're falling behind. But the truth? Most moms are quietly battling the same guilt — wondering if what they're doing is enough.

You are not alone in these feelings.
 But you don't have to live stuck in them.

God is not keeping score. He's offering grace.

Let your guilt turn your heart toward God. Let it be a reminder that you are not meant to carry the weight of motherhood alone. He is your strength. Your rest. Your wisdom. Your constant help in every moment.

Your children need a present mama, not a perfect one.

And the best thing you can do for them? Keep showing up. Keep bringing your worries to Jesus. Keep parenting from a place of grace, not guilt.

You are raising eternal souls, and God is with you in that holy work — even when dinner is drive-thru and screen time stretches too long.

Today's Prayer

Dear Father,

You see me. You see the moments I hide from the world — the ones where I feel like I'm failing.

You see the fast food wrappers on the counter, the tears behind my tired eyes, and the heaviness I carry in my heart.

Thank You for meeting me in the mess. Thank You that I don't have to be perfect to be loved.

Lord, remind me daily that I am not raising my children alone.

You are here — in every diaper change, every carpool, every meltdown, and every mealtime prayer.

Forgive me for the times I let guilt drown out Your truth.
Forgive me for the days I strive in my own strength instead of resting in Your grace.
Help me remember that even when I fall short, You never do.
When I feel like I'm not enough, remind me that You are more than enough for both me and my children.
Teach me to receive Your grace and to pass it on — especially to myself.
Fill my home with peace that comes from knowing I'm walking with You, one step at a time.
Let my children remember not a perfect mother, but a mother who loved deeply, repented quickly, and relied entirely on You.

In Jesus' name,

Amen.

2 Corinthians 12:9

But He said to me, "My grace is sufficient for you, for my power is made perfect in weakness." Therefore I will boast all the more gladly of my weaknesses, so that the power of Christ may rest upon me.

Psalms 94:19

In the multitude of my anxieties within me, Your comforts delight my soul.

Day 28

Surrender Control

Let's talk about something many moms struggle with—control.

Not in a domineering or bossy way, but in the quiet, everyday moments where we feel like the only way to get it done right... is to do it ourselves.
The laundry needs to be folded a certain way.
The dinner has to be just right.
The baby's schedule, the school forms, the packed lunches— we want it all done correctly. And that "correctly" usually means *our way.*

I'll be the first to admit: I struggle with letting others help.
Letting go feels like inviting in mistakes.
It feels inefficient. Risky.
But the truth is—when we cling to doing everything ourselves, we're not just shutting others out... we're often shutting God out, too.

We say, "I trust God,"
...but we won't let Him lead our days.
We say, "God's in control,"
...but we grip every detail of our homes, our children, and our future like it all depends on us.

But it doesn't.

Scripture reminds us that we were *never meant* to carry it all.
 "Cast your burdens on the Lord and He will sustain you…"
(Psalm 55:22)
 He doesn't expect us to be superwomen—He calls us to be surrendered women.

Think about Mary, the mother of Jesus. She surrendered her plans, her body, her entire future when she said yes to God. It wasn't convenient. It wasn't predictable. But it was faithful.

Or Moses' mother, Jochebed—who placed her baby in a basket and released him into a river. Can you imagine that moment? A mother letting go completely. But God honored her trust and raised Moses up to be a deliverer for His people.

Letting go is not weakness. It's worship.

We serve a God who sees more than we ever could. Who knows every outcome, every detail, every ripple effect. So when we try to control everything, we are relying on our limited human strength—rather than resting in His unlimited power.

We have to put aside the urge to do it all, fix it all, be it all— and instead turn to the One who *already is all*.

Today's Prayer

Father,

You know how tightly I hold on.
You see every moment I try to fix, manage, plan, or protect in
my own strength.
You see how hard it is for me to let others help—how I
whisper, "If I don't do it, it won't get done right."
But Lord, I'm realizing that even my best isn't always enough.
And You never asked me to carry it all.

So today, I surrender.
I surrender my plans. My schedule. My children. My
expectations.
I surrender the control that's wearing me down and the
pressure to do it all myself.
Help me trust You more—deeply and truly.
Teach me to rest in Your promises, not my performance.
Help me to give others room to help and to invite You into
every detail of my day.
Remind me that surrender is not giving up—it's giving over.
I choose today to give it over to You.

In Jesus' name,

Amen.

Proverbs 3:5-6

Trust in the Lord with all your heart and lean not on your own understanding; in all your ways submit to Him, and He will make your paths straight.

Isaiah 41:10

Don't be afraid, for I am with you. Don't be discouraged, for I am your God. I will strengthen you and help you.

Day 29

Let Them

This morning, my 3-year-old insisted on buckling her own car seat. If you've ever stood there, keys in hand, running late, you know the feeling. What takes me 3 seconds feels like an eternity when she's working so carefully with her little hands to be a big girl and buckle herself.

Every part of me wanted to reach over, click it in, and get on with our day. But as I stood there, shifting my weight and silently counting the seconds, I realized something: this was more than just a seatbelt. This was a teaching moment — not for her, but for me.

Sometimes, God uses these "slow-down moments" with our kids to remind us of what truly matters. We are so quick to rush through life, always moving to the next task, the next deadline, the next responsibility. But in those extra minutes, He is wanting us to: *Pause. Breathe. Be Present.*

It's the same when we let them "help" in the kitchen. Yes, it takes longer. Yes, there's flour all over them and the kitchen. But those little hands stirring batter or sprinkling flour are creating memories. To them, the mess doesn't matter. What matters is the time we give them.

Because children spell love T-I-M-E.

And here's the truth: our slowing down speaks louder than any lecture ever could. Without even saying a word, we're teaching them patience, presence, and unconditional love.

And when I stop to think about it, isn't that exactly how God loves us? Patiently. Gently. Giving us space to figure things out. He doesn't rush in to "fix it" the moment we struggle. He lets us try again, and again, and again — even when we stumble flat on our face the fourth time.

What feels like an eternity to us facing a struggle is actually grace. His grace. And when we model that with our children, we show them what God's love looks like in action.

So today, when it feels like forever watching your child try to tie their shoes, buckle their car seat, or stir the cookie dough — don't see it as wasted time. See it as an invitation. A reminder to slow down, to live in the moment, and to show God's love through your actions.

Today's Prayer

Lord,

Thank You for the gentle lessons You weave into everyday life through my children. When I'm tempted to rush, remind me that what feels like wasted minutes are actually sacred opportunities. Teach me to slow down, to savor these fleeting moments, and to see them as gifts rather than inconveniences.

Give me patience to wait, joy in the small things, and grace when life feels messy. Help me to love my children the way You love me — with endless patience, tender care, and time. May the way I pause and give them my presence be a reflection of how You are always present with me.

Strengthen me to show Your character in my actions, so my children may grow up not just hearing about Your love, but experiencing it through me.

In Jesus' name,

Amen.

Ephesians 4:2

Be completely humble and gentle; be patient, bearing with one another in love.

Psalm 86:15

But you, O Lord, are a compassionate and gracious God, slow to anger, abounding in love and faithfulness.

Day 30

I'm Sorry

There are moments in motherhood when the weight of our own humanity shows up loud and clear. We're tired. We've repeated the same instruction twenty times. We're trying to cook dinner while breaking up an argument in the next room. And then it happens — we snap. We raise our voices. We let frustration spill out.

Sometimes it looks like mom and dad bickering too loudly in front of the kids. Other times it's that moment when you see the hurt in their little eyes after something you said in a hurry. Maybe you brushed them off when they wanted to show you something, or maybe your words cut a little deeper than you realized in the moment.

These moments sting, don't they? And yet, they are also an opportunity. Because while pride tells us to brush it off and hope they forget, love — and the example of Christ — call us to stop, kneel down, and say the simple words: *"I'm sorry."*

Apologizing to our children doesn't make us weak. It makes us real. It shows them that even mom and dad need grace, and it paints a living picture of repentance and restoration. When we humble ourselves before them, we teach them that it is safe to admit when you're wrong. That humility is stronger than pride. That forgiveness restores what was broken.

The Bible reminds us: *"Confess your sins to each other and pray for each other so that you may be healed."* (James 5:16). That healing doesn't just happen in church pews — it begins in our homes. And Colossians 3:13 says, *"Bear with each other and forgive one another... Forgive as the Lord forgave you."* When our children see us practicing forgiveness, they begin to understand what God's grace really looks like in action.

Mama, every time you apologize, you are showing your children a piece of the Gospel. You're showing them that their mistakes won't push you away. You're teaching them that forgiveness is possible and that love can cover even the hardest of days.

What a gift it is to know that even in our failures, God can use us to point our children back to Him.

Today's Prayer

Lord,

Thank You for the precious gift of my children and for the ways You use even my mistakes to teach both me and them about Your grace. Too often I let my own frustrations, weariness, or impatience spill over in ways that hurt the little hearts You've entrusted to me. Forgive me for the times my words or actions have not reflected Your love.

Help me, Father, to walk in humility — to be quick to apologize when I am wrong and to show my children that repentance is not weakness, but strength. Teach me to model the same forgiveness that You so freely give to me every day. May my home be a place where grace flows easily, where healing comes through honesty, and where love covers over every shortcoming.

Lord, give me the patience to pause before I speak, the wisdom to build up rather than tear down, and the courage to admit when I fall short. Let my children see in me not a perfect parent, but a parent who points them to a perfect Savior. May the way I say "I'm sorry" open their hearts to know how deeply You love them, and may it teach them that no mistake is ever too big for Your forgiveness.

Thank You for never giving up on me. Help me never to give up on them.

In Jesus' name,

Amen.

Psalm 51:17

The sacrifice You desire is a broken spirit. You will not reject a broken and repentant heart, O God.

Luke 6:31

Do to others as you would have them do to you.

About the Author

Bethany Cloyd became a mother at the age of twenty, just a few short years after becoming a Christian. In many ways, she felt like a beginner in both. With a new baby in her arms and her faith still young, she often struggled with feeling unprepared and overwhelmed. The Bible, so big and unfamiliar, felt intimidating. Not having grown up reading or studying Scripture, she didn't know where to start. But out of her love for her children, she began with the simplest of steps—reading children's Bibles to them and learning alongside them.

Like so many mothers, Bethany quickly discovered that the busyness of life can so easily push spiritual priorities to the side. "I'll make time tomorrow" became a familiar phrase in her heart. Yet even in those seasons of slipping, God was at work. He was shaping her, teaching her, and pulling her closer to Him through the everyday trials and joys of motherhood.

Today, Bethany is living proof that there is hope and growth for anyone who feels behind in their walk with God. While she doesn't claim to be a perfect child of God, she has grown immensely since those early days. She now teaches children's Bible classes, leads women in Bible studies and VBS, and opens her family's home to her church regularly. Through all of this, her heart continues to beat strongest for her first mission field—her children.

When Bethany looks into the eyes of her children, she sees more than just little ones who need her care. She sees the Church of tomorrow. She sees the legacy she longs to leave behind—one of faith, love, and devotion to Christ. Her prayer is that her children, and the children of every mother who picks up this devotional, will grow to know, love, and serve the Lord with all their hearts.

Bethany wrote this devotional because she knows firsthand how many moms feel like they're not doing enough, don't know where to begin, or wonder if they're making any lasting impact at all. She wants moms to know that change doesn't come from perfection—it comes from small, faithful steps. Whether it's opening your Bible for a few minutes, reading a children's story Bible to get the basics under your belt, or simply showing up to worship with fellow believers, God uses it all.

Bethany's encouragement is this: you don't have to walk this road alone. You are not failing. And you are not unseen. God is working in your motherhood, and He will use your daily love and faithfulness to build His kingdom—for your children, for your family, and for generations to come.

Made in the USA
Middletown, DE
27 January 2026

27639532R00082